PLAYTIME

PLAYTIME

Andrew McMillan

CAPE POETRY

1 3 5 7 9 10 8 6 4 2

Jonathan Cape, an imprint of Vintage,
20 Vauxhall Bridge Road,
London SW1V 2SA

Jonathan Cape is part of the Penguin Random House group of companies
whose addresses can be found at global.penguinrandomhouse.com

Penguin
Random House
UK

First published by Jonathan Cape in 2018

penguin.co.uk/vintage

A CIP catalogue record for this book is available
from the British Library

ISBN 9781911214373

Typeset in 11/13 pt Bembo by Jouve (UK), Milton Keynes
Printed and bound in Great Britain by TJ International Ltd, Padstow, Cornwall

Penguin Random House is committed to a sustainable future for
our business, our readers and our planet. This book is made
from Forest Stewardship Council® certified paper.

for Ben

I would be born, and I would bear. Amen!

The Acts of John

CONTENTS

PLAYTIME

MARTYRDOM

tonight   I started walking back to you father
it was meant to be a stroll but then I started
walking faster   father   I started chanting all
the names of all the men I ever went to bed
with   father   my thighs were burning and my feet
were heavy with blood but I kept the pace and chants
of names up   father   listed them to fenceposts
and the trees and didn't stop and started getting
younger   father   and walked all night till I was home
just a spark in your groin again and told you not
to bring me back to life   told you I repented
every name and had freed them of me   father

I

I know a lot! I know about happiness! I don't mean the love of God, either: I mean I know the human happiness with the crimes in it.
Even the happiness of childhood.

Harold Brodkey

PLAYTIME

it will take a good ten minutes for them to stop
breathing as heavy as they are   for the burning
in their lungs to dampen   for the mud from the yard
to be trodden down into the hairbrown carpet

one boy clutches his chest as though trying to keep
his bones from bursting out   later he will ask me
how many tattoos I have   whether I have one
on my bum   whether he can look to verify

my denial   such innocence   such freedom in asking
for the body of another   I point him back
to the page   there will be time for him   for them all
to learn of the body's curve into awkwardness

to find their way into the rules and the lessons
they will come to know by heart   once   some schoolgirls
of ten or eleven   in my primary   drew
red crayon down a tampon   and left it hanging

half out of one of their schoolbags in the cloakroom
trying to rush themselves to adolescence
the girls in this class are huddled in the corner
having already learnt they should be suspicious

of new men   their necks seem longer than the boys'
they've learnt to hold themselves   they've learnt what small
words from them can do   there was a storeroom
in my primary school and if we were chosen

to tidy away mats after PE lessons
me and another boy would try out wrestling moves
on each other   the last time I remember it
we were both laid out on the mats after a slam

my body over his   cheap shorts almost touching
and I felt a warmth   nothing wet or sexual
something like light spreading across a cold surface
and a small part of the back corridor

of my mind is still lit by that moment   his eyes
on mine for longer than they should have been
seeing in them the whole incident   the grappling
amongst the quoits and plastic footballs   the fall

onto the mats   the staledinner breath   the knowing
then of what it was   of what it would be   soon

FIRST TIME

before the early times   finishing
in old socks or on my own belly
to feel the puddled temporary

warmth   there was the first time   and before
even that   there were the shameful years
of not knowing what it was   or why

I'd wake each morning   sure
I'd wet myself   and find myself dry
but larger than the night before   why

the piss fizzed as it hit the bowl
why I always shrank back down to size
what the other boys were laughing at

in school   why they would brag how many
times a day they did it   why the men
at football games would move their hands like that

and then that night of discovery
an October holiday   Blackpool
because my granddad had recently died

and grandma wanted the family
together   the sea couldn't rest
and the empty slots of days dropped down

in front of us each morning   one night
when it felt as though the whole hotel
was asleep   I reached down and tented

the floral covers on my single bed
a few quiet strokes   and then a tide
a pool a bursting through my joggers

and I ran to the bathroom   I hadn't
reckoned on the stuff that lingers after
the smell   the taut body's fear of being

caught   it didn't feel pleasurable
more like learning a secret you could
forget and learn again each day

I went back to bed   hoping the night
might dry me as I sank down into
my given task   mourning what had passed

GLIMPSE

on the pitch by my house   the weekly game
of football   there was one lad   already
famous in our class for having snogged a girl
and still my friend   despite the pull
of the pack mentality I always felt
outside of   I had no skill   could only
put my body in front of someone else
in hopes of slowing them for a moment
and this time it caused my friend to fall
and   in the split second it took for him
to regain himself   I saw   slipped
from shorts and briefs   his whole private self
though he hadn't noticed   still giggling
at my sudden prowess at defence
and after that   there were other times   crowding
into a friend's bedroom   me pretending
not to look as someone showed himself
to a girl   and the emptiness that followed
nobody yet ready to do the things
that come after   though it was still deliberate
and so different from that earlier time
the grass   that glimpse of something that seemed
to be all potential   tiny sapling
not yet seeding   just another part
of our innocence   fear and lust and shame
not yet ripened to full blush

CURTAIN

we were above the stage in a corridor
I was due on next to fool my way
through a singing part   I can't remember
if he worked there   or what his role could have been

I know I wanted him to help me into
the trousers   liked the way his hands smoothed
the leather   maybe the end of the run
made him brave   *lets take a look at what you've got*

he   I don't want to say asked   requested?
the way an audience can request an encore
pulling it out of you from that deep part
beneath the ribs that doesn't want to disappoint

when I was sixteen I wanted so much
to please   would steal any scene for laughs
and so I did   pulled down the yfronts my mum
had bought for me   and let it hang like a rope

is that all you've got he said   and didn't ask
for more   and it hung there in the backstage cold
like something already dead   and I bowed
and pulled up   and stepped out   and performed

THINGS SAID IN THE CHANGING ROOM

I don't still carry them on my shoulders
I think   probably   they're rested somewhere
in the scoop of my clavicle   the time
a teacher shamed my obese body
as I pulled my shirt over my head

or the time a new young supply teacher
seemed to look at me with pity   as though
my body was someone else's misbehaving child
so each time I'd take myself to the edge
of the tiled square   away from splintered benches

the whole thing no bigger than a modest
corner shop and full of my classmates
the two types of bodies boys that age have
the flabby   baggy ones   the skin a shirt
draped over them they're trying to grow into

or the ones thin as bunsen flame   who seemed
embarrassed by their own fragility
all waiting for the body to exert
itself over its own boundaries
some boys knew how to make a performance

of their size   my instinct was to hide
not shower   let the acrid stink of sweat
and nylon settle on my skin   the ones
skinny enough to be able to pretend muscle
would take their time   do slow circuits

of the group   hold eye contact with everyone
over half of them have children now
where before I'd think of them undressing

for their wives   now I'm kept awake by thoughts
of them as fathers   what they're thinking

as they bath their sons   how they will tell them
the stories of their bodies   what soft curves
they've built to hide the minor injuries
of marriage   which parts have grown slower
which parts of them ache as they lift their boy out

to get the body of their favourite sports star
they must starve themselves   that the muscles
are there already   if they could only
get at them   that the thing to do is eat less
and replace meals with water   so that they bloat
and then feel their insides flushing out

that the stomach will expand and shrink back
like a gas holder in a former
industrial town   that once the body
has burned off all its fat   it will start on muscle
that more exercise just gives more energy
for the body to eat itself alive

that they can forget what it's like to stand
without feeling dizzy   that their eyesight
can fail   that their salad can be carried
in smaller and smaller tupperware boxes
that the doctor will be forced
to ban the gym   will deliver his prognosis

that they will end up in the carpark of the doctors
with their mum saying *imagine   a child of mine   malnourished*

FIRST TIME 'POSH'

how many other young lads did this   took
themselves to bed in order to prepare
for the real thing   like pregnancies
in the dark ages   the self shut away
only to emerge empty yet somehow
more important   the body that is only
true in private   the undressing the legs
slightly raised   the pinch and roll that feels
almost surgical   then afterwards
something like peeling back a stocking
a possible life seeping out the end
you didn't know to knot before binning
the tiny deaths you would come to know
the smell of and their ghoststains on the sheets

TO THE CIRCUMCISED

and what happened to their foreskins
afterwards   perhaps thrown in the rubbish   dumped
in landfill   or incinerated   maybe
and now just dust on someone's office chair

and what difference between the ones who have
it done when they're babies   before they know
the significance of what's been cut   and the ones
who   turned sixteen   find the foreskin too tight

for their urges   trying to breathe
in a shirt done up to the collar
when the collar is too small   and how these boys must
force themselves to tell their parents   then show

a doctor   then a nurse   how they must feel
like someone who is trying to prove the fault
with a product they are wanting to return
and what of the ultra orthodox ones

who   as newborns   had the blood sucked from the tips
of their fresh cut cocks by the Mohel   what do they
remember as they grow up missing a piece
of themselves that could   they might come to think

have protected them   and the ones who lose it
when they're older   do they mourn it more for having
known it   for being able to remember the gas
that forced them into sleep   being woken roughly

and their whole flaccid boyhoods wrapped in blue
spongy gauze   and do they still hold their memories

of each time getting hard being agony
of getting used to the absence

its true it had not been of use to them
but how extravagant they must have felt
to have a part of themselves that had no purpose
or was not fit for purpose   but still had its place

TRANSPLANT

the sound of hair being ripped out
reminded me of velcro shoes
being hastily removed   I hadn't
realised it possible
that I might grow into kinder
ownership of my own looks
that I could   one day   have been fine
with baldness   but it seemed to me
at seventeen that I was being
unmanned   and that my unlived youth
was already receding
so I paid a doctor thousands
to take a strip of hair from the back
of my head   pull out each follicle
and put them into the front
to give me the line I thought would
make me happy   and stitch the skin
on the back of the skull together
leaving me with this grimace
this equator   this scar
that catches the cold weather   holds
it deep inside   reminder
of my vanity   tideline
of Canute   tattoo of the time
I couldn't live with what I was becoming

FIRST TIME WITH FRIENDS

having just learnt of the pleasures the body
can give itself   I am waiting for the rest
of the tent to fall asleep   they should be tired
having spent the whole day being taught how to surf

I didn't get the hang of it   hadn't dared
to stand   rode in each cresting wave on my knees
while my classmates seemed born to ride them out
already able to lock their legs   use their core

we hung our wetsuits on the tentpoles   teachers
jokingly asking if we'd pissed in them   later
lit by dusk   the suits become an audience
peering into us   that's what I decide on

for fantasy   as I slip my hand inside
the sleeping bag   use the other to force a space
to work in   and trying to stay silent   check
my friends' snores are still in rhythm with the wind

on the canvas   its only afterwards
someone's breath seems to falter   perhaps smelling
something familiar   and afraid his body
has betrayed him again   we don't mention it

as we slip our wetsuits back on the next day
I squeeze myself in   suddenly aware
of the lumps and curves of my adolescent
frame   as the waves arch their backs far out at sea

we prepare ourselves for another lesson
this one on bravery   how in open water
the swell that seems as though it could overwhelm you
can come to break as almost nothing on the shore

JOCASTA

before I do   let me tell you what I've learned
you still have to wake up and carry on
I hadn't really mourned my husband much
before this young one arrived inside the gates

his penetration went so deep inside
it felt like a returning   something coming
home   I think I worked it out before he did
but I had missed him all these years   and missed

my husband   the brain is not logical
the body is not a desert   even as
we age   when he learnt the truth he looked repulsed
part of me had always thought all men desired

to re-enter the chamber of their birth
that war was just a symptom of their rage
at not being able to   well my boy
licked the sides I'd pushed him through   found the nipples

I'd fed him with   and couldn't live with what
he'd done   so now my loverson has empty
breadbaskets for eyes   and his father has
a shallow grave outside the city walls

and so I've learnt to trust only what I have
in this one small room   this square of light
this handful of neck   this noose   this table
this one short step

WITH CHILD

before my birth   my mother walked with concrete
animals   two hours before that she'd pulled
into the hard shoulder   a headache boring
through her skull   nine months before that she'd made
tea   heavy with the weight of knowing something
had been done   sat to eat as tension misted at the windows
and one morning   having carried me almost
full term   my mother sat up in bed   saying
with an uncommon strength   that they had to drive
north   to the park with the life-sized animal
sculptures   and she wouldn't say why   except
it felt right   the unborn son with the whole life
ahead   the animals who would weather better
live longer than her   and would still be there
when their warmblooded relatives were extinct

PATERNUS

it feels voyeuristic
seeing it here on the street
windtossed nest   small down lingering
between the fingers of the twigs
seeming somehow dense but light
like a gathering of private
hair   shorn off in preparation
for the letting go of someone

I am thinking of my mother
of my sister   who is pregnant
for the second time   of all
the empty rooms in the city
of patience   of waiting for a birth
of these tiny eggs at my feet
of this being one less time the shell
will crack   life will shudder out   hungry

DEATH DREAM

I am six and walking in the woods
with my dad   someone has died or been told
they are dying   and I am taken away
drama unfolds in the trees ahead
but every time it burns itself out
before we reach it   only the aftermath
the hound   its mouth in the open purse
of the stomach   the hot wet stink around its lips
the fox an empty robe laid out on the ground
neck broken   eyes ripened from their sockets
and   either side of the brokenbridgespine
the synapses are fizzing   like a bulb
about to lose the last of its light

FIRST TIME SEXTING

too young or shy for the real thing
I used the internet to find
another boy my age   both of us
old enough to know what we wanted
wasn't 'ordinary'   that no one
taught it us in schools   but our bodies
seemed drawn towards this thing we couldn't
articulate   and so we described
it to each other   nightly   for hours
what we imagined it might be
what we knew our bodies could do alone
whether they could do the same with
someone else   for months we texted that way
in different schools   hiding at the back
of different English lessons   naming
the places we thought we'd like to meet
each other   which   in truth   were places
we were used to being with ourselves
our bedrooms   the shower cubicle
then   one day   in the rush for lunch
I left my phone out on a table
and someone read the contents to the Year
and I stepped back into a room
covered in the ooze of a secret
split open   and their faces were
red with it   I could see the secret dripping
from their lips   and I grabbed my mobile
which you'd think I'd say was heavier
but it felt lighter somehow   and I ran
outside   and cried   and for the first time ever
refused to go to class

and my phone sat vibrating
in my pocket   like a heartbeat
refusing to be silent   maybe
halfwanting to be discovered

WATCHING THE STUDENTS

they know I am not of their time   I am
to them a jug of water with a meal
something they need but don't notice   a glass
through which they want to see themselves   I can't
show them anything   tell them what I want to
of their beauty   it is something they must
learn in negotiation with each other
there is nothing I could ever ask for
except for this one chance to watch them
on a quiet afternoon   they are
so lonely for love   they can't be alone
they wander the grounds to find each other
they sit arguing the terms of how
their bodies will exist together
how they will survive the knowing of each other

FIRST TIME PENETRATION

we needed two attempts   the first time
was so cold   in the unheated loft room
of a friend's house I'd moved to at sixteen
that all we could do was force our bodies
close enough to save a little heat

the second time   I planned a little more
a portable heater kicking out
a charred dust smell   leading him upstairs
the room artificially hot   stripping
off instantly   how practical I was

not really wanting to be touched   or kissed
or to do anything that might delay
what I thought I needed   heater unplugged
the room dropping colder almost instantly
walking to the bed   kneeling down on it

as though praying   and him coming at me
with his bare inarticulate thrusting
that couldn't hold off long enough for pain
to give way into something like pleasure
and I remember feeling something drip

I've left a present on your back he said
and I showed him out   past the bedroom
of my housemate   the bed I'd taken
to sleeping in most mornings   when she'd gone
early to the station   I'd set the bath

running and keep warm under the covers
still muggy with her presence   one time
I fell asleep   woke to water coming

through the ceiling   as though the sky had slipped
inside the house   and I just lay there

not moving   thinking there was nothing
to be done but wait for it to pass through
the different layers of house   hope it might
dry out   might still be standing afterwards

PERSONAL TRAINER

remember   first the body must be bruised
so it can heal itself stronger   tense your stomach
I am going to punch you as though you were
a weight bag   I'll hit your sleeping abdominals
force them awake   I will punch you   though I know
you've never been punched before   smacked yes
on your wrist or your arse to reprimand you
as a child   but never someone wanting
to hurt you   I will punch you so your body
grows more resilient   so it learns the centre
of its own gravity   I will punch you
until you go slack   and then I'll send you home
in the morning you will ache   you will feel
as though you have been trodden on   standing
or sitting will require you to fold yourself
like a hinge   your muscles will not yet be ready
to be stretched   this will last for days   until
you're ready to be punched again   it is
in this way I will build you   your abs screwing
tighter every week   holding themselves closer
to the surface of the skin   like the knuckles
of a fist which is being clenched   and pushed forwards

MAKING WEIGHT

some of the self must be cut down before the fight
which means this ritual of icebath
and then laying on the bed   swaddled
like someone ready to be sacrificed
and then back into the cold water
and repeat   three times   or taking laxatives
to help the self lighten   while a friend sitting
in the bedroom pretends he can't recognise
the smell of everything not vital
to the body's survival being emptied
distracts himself thinking of the other
young man in his bedsit north of the city
who has not got far enough towards the weight
and so is trying to bulk rapidly
who is eating two three times his own mass
who it's possible to imagine eating whole
chickens   cows   like a sideshow attraction
at a carnival   so by the time both meet
at the match they are surprised to see
they look the same   that each has been working
to ensure they'd meet in the ring as equals
both of them trying to be a slightly better
version of the other   and now   waxed hairless
almost naked   and their friends at ringside
who have given up some pounds   and want a show

WATCHING MMA

having booked a hotel in a town with the same name
in the wrong state   and the Amtrak already leaving
into the hills   I checked in to a Howard Johnson
it was as if they'd built the motel   the church next door
then moved the town ten miles down the road   I ordered
takeaway pizza and turned on the TV   hurried
through the local news and preachers to the sport   where two
caged men were going to fight until one of them lay
unconscious   or tapped out   or one of them landed enough
strikes against the other to be awarded more points
the match started like any drunken scrap
each flirting with the space between each other   a few
punches to the air for range   and then taking it down
to the mat   and for the longest time they seemed to lay
on top of one another   jerking suddenly
writhing like a fleshcoloured bag of small animals
and if you ignored the clenched fists   the costumes   the head
split like a yoghurt pot and leaking   if you forgot
the cage   the phlegm dragged up from the lungs by exertion
the empty look in the eyes of the defeated man
they could have been lovers   reuniting

BOXING BOOTH

i

if you haven't got a ring   rope off
a square of land   before you've even fought
you have to set the stage   and draw the crowd
let the spieler list your reputation
as though this were your eulogy
see which young man volunteers   so earnest
as though he has waited his whole young life
to prove himself   let him wait awhile
against the ropes and posts you'd use
to tether horses   let the crowd's shouts
flay him where he stands   let the anger
make him dizzy   then ring the bell

ii

imagine being Gregor   waking
one morning to find that Kafka has
transformed you   you've lost your agency
can only scrabble for bits of flesh
with the pads on your insect feet
like trying to pick something up
in boxing gloves   all limbs suddenly
angular   as though broken   and you
might   in a wet throated buzz   try
articulating why it was you
were chosen as a symbol that men
equate power with the suffering
of others   why it is when men look down
at the fraying cloth of their hearts
their instinct is to mend it with their hands

when the young pretender has been floored
and you've scrambled for the loose coins
with a red   torn   large ham hock of a hand
it's time to take down the show   and move
it on   how quickly the ruckus
in the dirt is brushed clean over
how quickly things can be dismantled
and the violence held inside dispersed
except a buzzing that hangs heavy
in the air   seems to follow you home
seems to be coming from inside of you
and wakes you each day before dawn   fresh
from dreaming of fists and teeth and weeping
and   slick with the shame of what you've done
you reach under the sheets   find yourself changed

II

it be right that the men who have benefited us should be called gods

The Acts of John

PRAISE POEM

last night you sang to my body
praised every inch of it
made it feel rare and royal
spoke to it the way you might speak
to a child in need of self
esteem   taking time on each part
the mouth and the tongue
the nipples and the chest
praising the severity
of the circumcision   and how
I talked to the older couple
in the bar who had been praising
my father   I'd thought my body
dull and base   I'd thought it loose
and wilted from the weight loss
but you composed hymns to it
cleaned it   bowed down before it
as though it might save you

BLOOD

we could be gathered for the reading of a will
each of us wanting to learn what it is
we have inherited from the one who loved
or did not love us   the nurse calls me in
for bloods   says she could get it from a stone   wraps
my upper arm   taps the inside of my elbow
as though it is a trunk she is trying to coax
sap from   I close my eyes   and when I open them
it's done   sitting mottled in its canister
and there are the questions to be answered
yes I know the risks associated and *yes*
once   he was Brazilian   yes I did ask
positive   no protection   when I leave
I feel a dread moving in that will not lift
for two weeks   settling down to the front
of my skull   until the text comes through
and I am light again   having put my ear
to the dense secrets of my blood   and heard nothing
but the curious weight which has been passed down
through the generations of this family
to know how close to us the dead are sitting
and to believe we honour them best by living

INHERITANCE

you call me to task   roll onto your stomach
without a word from you I know to take my tongue

and run it the length of your back   base of spine
to ears   where the teeth will let themselves be heard

its not a straight line that does it   but rather
random lappings   like spots of rain before a storm

it is something I was told by someone else
who showed me on my own back   when it's done right

it sends a feeling of surprise towards
the neck   escaping as brief moans   and so it is

I pass it on   and isn't this what humankind
was made for?   telling stories   learning where the skin

is most in need of touch   teaching   as we ourselves
were taught   of pleasure

DAMP

the day you left for good   I let you fall
onto the quilt   made you keep
the football shirt on   started
where the hem rode up from the boxer rim
and drew my wet tongue up from the sponsor
to the crest   up past the logo
of the kit designer   to your armpit
where the smell like wet leaves drew me in
deeper   and the musk and hair seemed like all
of the mulched world   half hidden by the cuff
of the sleeve   and the tongue never quite
getting in   and the rain impatient at the window
and your eyes never quite wanting to meet mine

SKIRT

what possessed us?   heads flipflopped from the wine
the food so posh it needed commentary
from the waitress   each dish turned inside out
split into pieces   then   stumbling home
the stars so low they could have been driving
towards us   getting back   we began

the loose fall into each other that drink
always induces   the body too soft
to pull or hold   once we'd spun into the bedroom
I stepped back   requesting each item
taken off in turn   the shoes   the jacket   the shirt
each one flung with performed indifference

for the bottom half you'd gone for trousers
with a skirt over the top   to recall
the flavour of some catwalk show   I chose
the trousers next   left the skirt on you   the pleats
just long enough to cover your cock
and belted at your thin blades of stomach hair

your drunk   imperfect body in a skirt
moving with each swaying breath   looking like
some ancient tribesman   in something someone
might have fashioned out of leaves   to give room
for dancing   to give space to the body
for its speechless articulation of thanks

SPIT

there are the men who like being spat on
long slow drool   from someone knelt above them
like honey pouring itself over
the edge of a spoon into a warm bowl

I think asking someone to degrade you
is about wanting to know the body
is a solid presence in the room
it has stumbled into   where the shy nectar

will be quick and heavy from their mouth
into yours   there are things in my life
I did not handle well   like the man
I slept with twice   who found out he was

Positive   and the third time   as I felt
my body pull towards him   I stopped
and asked instead if he knew when   or who
he didn't   and described years of anonymity

in bars   of wanting so much to step out
of his own mind he threw his body
into crowds   pain being able to make us
forget our thoughts   momentarily

though the morning after   laying in bed
stilled from too much of too much   there is
the slow return of wetness to your mouth
the one reminder that you are still alive

MAKING LOVE

home before you   and wanting to start something
after weeks of petty fights and only touching
accidentally or when sleeping   I grabbed
your laptop from the table   went straight for
the internet history   knowing that if
familiarity had unsexed me I could
find something to shock us back together
and I did   and kept my arousal at halfpower
until you came back   then threw you straight onto
the floor   and pulled you up   carried you to bed
and dropped you there like an unwanted present
and if someone had asked me what your name was
at that point I don't think I could have remembered
there was only the moment I was trying
to give you   the half open door of the laptop
your face pressed into the blank screen of the pillows
the evening sun setting the neighbourhood on fire

MAKING UP

those times when sex is an apology
when *sorry* isn't a word   but giving
the whole self over to the other one
who has been wronged   or thinks they have been wronged

it is mostly less selfish   not able
to show that you want anything other
than to prove how cruel you have been
how much you have hated being hated

and to the thigh   the crotch   the chest   you ask
with everything you have   to be allowed back
it is nothing new   but you do it
as if for the first time   before

your bodies were ordinary to each other
and now   it is precisely because
what you have to offer is so humble
that it makes you so much easier to forgive

ANAPHORA PENISES

I disagree with you on this
one small point   the time you said   of penises
when you've seen one you've seen them all I think

you're wrong   each one is fingerprint unique
each with its own way of being in the world
shy or all bravado or statesmanlike

it's not size   though you can feel each one trying
to push itself upright   like a schoolboy
hoping to be called on to give an answer

it's smaller things   the smell of each one   the way
the day can linger there   beneath the slim lips
of the foreskin   each with its own direction

each with its own personality   its own
way of introducing itself   each of them
a personal totem for the bearer

each its own low pendulum marking the passing
of each year with its own minutiae
of successes/changes/health scares   each one

of singular importance to each singular
man   each treasured and wept for and prone
to misjudgement   and not to be trusted

CLEARANCE

there is a type of sex your mother would
never want for you   one where you don't kiss
where you barely touch   where a friend comes round
to empty your life of your ex
and ends up on their knees   amongst the cups
and birthday cards which have already
come to seem trivial   it is not
what she would have hoped for when you were young
this selfishness   this greed   this rush to be
empty   she had always taught you to be
gentle   to put others before yourself
to give people a second chance   she would
not have imagined there could be this side
to you   she raised you so much better

PHONEBOX

the rain was a sudden unexpected caller
to the street   the type that comes immediately

no prior drizzled suggestion of itself   just
downpour   and the phonebox was the only shelter

and it seemed to welcome me   somehow larger
as though grateful for another use   beyond

the frantic drug scores and weeping drunks locked out
of the station   the rain's taptapping fingers

were relentless on the glass   my bus not due
for ten more minutes   when he appeared

clothes heavy and clinging like wet armour
he looked so miserable I let him enter   offered

the space as though I lived there   he squeezed in
perhaps deciding it would be less awkward

if we didn't face each other   we both kept our
eyes on the sky   reading it for any signs

of a break   a puddle formed at his feet
as he dripped dry   the back of his suit trousers

slowly let go of the outline of his boxers
and for a moment   as he stepped back from a truck's

loud grumble   I felt the whole weight of him
pressed up against me   and when he stepped forward

my clothes had patches of water where he'd been
small lakes of him resting in the seams

to a passerby we might have looked like lovers
ready to be buried together   but before

I could even ask his name   or make some joke
about the small wings his wet shoulder blades had left

on my chest   the sky relit itself   and he left
our shelter without speaking   as easily

as someone who had tried to make a call
but found the line dead   as they'd hoped it would be

LAST TRAIN

the threeseaters have become beds
for the last workers out of Sheffield
one young man reclines as if
in a sauna   when the heat has loosened
the body   and the balls are at their lowest
what would it be to lay with him
naked as a navvy   to lick him dry
of the day he's had   to be still with him
as the night outside hardens down to coal

WORKMAN

be a welcoming host   serve him
coffee   keep out of his way
noise is how he lets you know
he's useful   learn to embrace it
do not resent the dust   think of it
as all his sweat made solid   run
your finger through it   put out your tongue
and feel the roughness of his trade
offer him more coffee   ask him
about his wife   when he raises
his hands to the top shelf
he is mending   try not to look
too obviously   as his shirt
prises its way out of its tuck
and shows a belly   midway between
muscled and beer

I know what work is   it is
the completing of a thing half-done
something   perhaps   that you started
but failed at   and so had to ask
for help   when he comes it is because
you have called him   open your door
he will be dressed brazenly
in paint and the rubble of his labours
invite him in   ask him to take
his shoes off   shake his hand   point him
towards the place where he is needed

DANCER

even sitting here in this cafe   his body
seems tense   as if at any moment the eye
might pass something to the brain which would require
an explanation with the limbs   he never
lets his joints relax into their socketgrooves
each movement the beginning of a potential
work of art   he is alert   even after rehearsal
when I invite him back to the flat to shower
before that night's performance   he moves through
the rooms so carefully   as though deciding
a way to best inhabit them   I'd imagined
he would be too beautiful to be curious
but each shelf and photo receives his audience
of wet hair   tight body where each part's connection
to another part is visible   his battered
feet leaving their notations on the false wood floor
his silent   transitory music playing
out beyond my ability to follow

PRIEST

forgive me   I know that I am staring
it's just I had thought devotion
to another made one plain   but you

dear Father   have taken your body
as the rough clay of its beginning
seen it as your duty to sculpt it

your tight black shirt a public prayer
to the beauty of creation   dog collar
stretched around a neck grown thick from lifting

in the gym   and you're reading   *When God Talks Back*
a page or two   then wandering the cafe
table to table   seeming to know

each customer by name   everyone
who we believe when they say
that they have spoken to God goes on

to head a congregation   which must mean
that God is telling them that he is lonely
I go to the bathroom   wait outside

as a girl convenes with herself
whilst the tap runs   I watch two students
approach you   ask loudly if you can explain

the Anglican approach to   something   the end of what
is lost beneath the steam hiss
of coffee machines   you seem able

to reassure them   I suppose
that is what people want from religion
to ask of someone else things they would not ask

of one another   the girl emerges
wringing her hands to dry them   you go back
to your book   I wonder

if there is a chapter on shyness
on disguising yourself as a bush
setting it aflame   or the murder

of your only Son   the ways we might
draw people towards us   the lengths the Lord
might go to   to have someone to speak to

LOCAL TRAIN

take   for example   the boy opposite
his body like a river which has not yet gathered
the rain it takes to learn the limits of the self
are malleable   a single unbroken curve

from the underside of his jaw to his spread legs
the things which age him at late teenage are debris
caught on him from someone else's life   the nose ring
the slight moss of hair on his arms and his stomach

as he takes a gym bag bigger than his torso
from the luggage rack   oh to be that young again!
to have a body not yet dragged and creased by age
to be as slight and brief of flesh   to be a man

without the heaviness it brings   to be able
to feel where each of the bones meets the skin   to still
be learning how deep the waters of desire
can run   to be unafraid of drowning

INTIMATES

I'm wearing your underwear to the office
after a long fortnight of working
and not enough time to sort and wash
the stains that mark our progress through a day

I want to make a kink from this necessity
but don't get how   is it that undressing
later you'll see something of yourself
on me and want it back?   is it that I've taken

without asking   and this slight transgression
reframes me as a stranger?   is it
something about simply feeling closer?
the rub of the other against the self

in their absence?   I feel none of that
as I pull the boxers from a pile
where each identical pair smell of detergent
and are slightly too small for my body

which has spread   through comfort   since you moved in
but all day something of yours is hugging
close to the worst parts of myself   less than
a year ago   I could not have imagined
the possibility of something so wonderful

TRAIN

of course there is always another one
like him   skin only barely able to conceal
the angles of the skull   looking as though
he is being told off   his eyes cast down
to *The Book of Sleep*   there's always
someone like him   the beauty of his face
its clean lines   and then sudden disturbance
of a cough that seems to come up
from the same place that hunger does
and his arm across the mouth to cover
it   like a wrestler   like someone being
mugged   tonight I'll lay awake thinking
of him   his grey eyes open
in another city   I hope he'll be
cured of his afflictions   in this life
I have chosen to love only one man
and I am still in search of evidence
to prove that this was not a wrong idea

I would flee, and I would stay. Amen

The Acts of John

RETURNING

over each other like hastilystacked chairs
digging further into one another
pulling back the balls   and scrotum   and nosing
through the brackentrail to your anus   I am
trying to stay in the moment   not consider
the human desire to consume what it loves
that it must have something to do with
containing the world   its perfect roundness
folded into the dark   and crawling with you
back towards this most base of our needs   to taste
something of the foul swamp of our origin
to bring our faces to the door through which
all disgust and pleasure is in hiding
from the abandonments   the wet streets
the unrelenting ugliness of this world

NOTES & ACKNOWLEDGEMENTS

'first time   posh' uses 'posh' in the euphemistic sense to mean masturbating whilst wearing a condom

'Jocasta' reconsiders the eponymous mother's life after Oedipus' death

'with child' describes the Brankston Cement Menagerie

'boxing booth' is thinking of the boxing matches that would tour with Fairgrounds   a spieler is someone who introduced each fighter to the crowd

'damp' is for Zaffar Kunial   though not about him

thanks to Dan and Lucy for their generosity in letting me use their cottage where many of these poems were written or edited

thanks to Robin Robertson   for his generosity   insight and intelligence in editing this manuscript

thanks to Seán Hewitt who always read bad drafts so diligently   and to others   Fiona Benson   Antony Dunn   Niven Govinden   Sarah Hymas   Helen Mort   Okey Nzelu   Helen Tookey who read these poems so patiently

thanks to the following publications where previous versions of these poems appeared *Adroit Journal Ambit Cake Cent Granta Hwaet: 20 years of Ledbury Poetry Festival Lambda Literary Literary Review New Boots and Pantisocracies New Statesman The North Oxford Poetry Poems in Which Poetry Poetry London Poetry Review The Reader The Scores The Valley Press Anthology of Yorkshire Poets White Review Wordlife Anthology* some were first broadcast on BBC Radio 3 & 4